EVEN SHORN

SARABANDE BOOKS
Louisville, KY

even

shorn

isabel

duarte-gray

Library of Congress Cataloging-in-Publication Data

Names: Duarte-Gray, Isabel, author.
Title: Even shorn / poems by Isabel Duarte-Gray.
Description: First edition. | Louisville, KY: Sarabande Books, 2021
Identifiers: LCCN 2020016781 (print) | LCCN 2020016782 (e-book)
ISBN 9781946448743 (paperback; acid-free paper)
ISBN 9781946448750 (e-book)

Subjects: LCSH: Elegiac poetry. | LCGFT: Poetry.
Classification: LCC PS3604.U246 E94 2021 (print)
LCC PS3604.U246 (e-book) | DDC 811/.6—dc23
LC record available at https://lccn.loc.gov/2020016781
LC e-book record available at https://lccn.loc.gov/2020016782

Cover and interior design by Alban Fischer.
Printed in Canada.
This book is printed on acid-free paper.
Sarabande Books is a nonprofit literary organization.

This project is supported in part by an award from the
National Endowment for the Arts. The Kentucky Arts Council,
the state arts agency, supports Sarabande Books with state tax dollars
and federal funding from the National Endowment for the Arts.

Contents

I

Night Jar

my red dress color
of a dairy barn
the pretty cows it
holds the winter berry and the brightest
bird who stays to eat we go
it's me and you the
time the lightning bugs
hang low above their
carrot flower candles like a
angel stopped to think a spell
me and you down to the barn to milk
our sheba in her dust cradle
when daytime's stole
the bucket gone too heavy please
hold onto me I hold your hem
my dress gone dark the red gone the
color of the backs of leaves
I see our stars through three-finger
oak and five-finger maple
tell mama how I lost my red
the gift she give me in my dress
and what to call it
now alone inside the sound of

walking in the night my dress
no color left at all

Driskill, Kentucky

Cutter Quilt

I.

the night river is a woman washing
clean the moon
upon forgiving rocks

II.

are these nails my person are they
dead apart of me the callus where
I grip my drawknife all my life
was pink as hatchlings or
a child born just a little
dead already tied and then I
waked to watch his afterbirth
be buried in a hole
in Tennessee

III.

cowslips are so named
to tell us where to watch the ground for shit
our fathers planted flags
carved out of sounds
carved flowers

IV.

here in winter

darkness finds

my hand trapped in the velvet

of the sumac and the velvet

of the antler

V.

a cat's tongue is a briar patch

a dog's tongue is a madstone

a snake's tongue is a trigger finger

Man's tongue pleases no one

VI.

when a dove is shot's the only time

to see her color true the way her color is

a hinge into the gray

rolls into fawn wades into

morning pink it's as if

speckles storming on the trout

caught in a basin

caught the light

VII.

the women beat the stains into the water

the river beats the stain into the land

Dycusburg, Kentucky

[I said your daddy's gone]

I said your daddy's gone
to buy a Cadillac runs smooth
as butterbeans
with salt

the bootlegger's worn him
to a knob of head
like a bone the dog unburied down
at Dycusburg

the girl they got was
a osage orange no
good to nobody but
to toss from one boy to the other
til she split
in two

to think you might drag a answer
out the river like a man drowned
no it don't mean it won't stray
past the edge of things
but words is words and men
just chew red plugs tucked in
their gums

I seen them running
liquor over Skinframe Creek
the engine rattling good as
his hands on bad days

I only hit my children
when they need it
to remember
but this man no man
could say his needs or tell
what hurt stuck inside him
like a tooth or thistle

I took the bottle
to his skull til I could take him
home again
to answer

Dycusburg, Kentucky

Chamber

nights we talk
the woman painted on his arm
before the Navy stole him
tells me what waters she seen
inside his dreams

back when my legs were like twigs
you'd bite into
to find the taste
of lemon this man
knew no words

I find him home odd hours
bottled up for later and before
I pass the shepherd at the door a ticking
like he got to chuckling with his dead he had
the pistol out but one bullet

which was fewer bullets
than my husband had
of wives

Princeton, Kentucky

Complaint

I am weary with my groaning
all the night I make my bed to swim
the minnows swallowed live to cure a cough
plodding still I tell of gravity
the curl of carp in shallow rivers sniffing
for the temperature of life
what are bones that they can feel
be vexed for stillness
as the wind prepares
to choose the word most carefully
for rain the silty dread
when rocks will slither
down the mountain in a saffron
scarf the rags of hillsides pool
into a pillow for my dreaming there is comfort
to be taken when two dreads are parted
should I drown my couch in tears

Murray, Kentucky

Even Shorn

time I lost my teeth I didn't think to mourn them
though the ache swung my jawbone
far across the ripplegrass

the Cadiz dentist give me
such a jar of new mouth as could
reincarnate mine

I'd as soon shake my ashes
loose on the cattail slough
the way you wait a death that's quick

Dresden, Tennessee

Like Hell You Are

The Devil made a meal of me and all
the Sundays I was sleeping.
To think of all the hours,
what I might've offered to the Book or of the Book
to needful ears grown up like burdock in our hag-rid
thorn-bit flock of town.

Sunday at the bedpost, heeling way
a good dog might, his face near a man's.
He kept a blade to pick his teeth, what fathers used
for supper fixed the way our mothers did,
hog meat from a creature slaughtered on the land.

Now I don't fix any man a meal like her,
and work it is to do it, though only one child mine to hush.
Her supper was a parting, like
to square it up with him and God,
what order seemed most right to her.
Did she even love them?

What I fixed was skin, thumbed good,
unbound, leafed through, like these
trees would free me something fresh, and
something came and gone without a word.

She was good when goodness penned her. Sparrow-loose
I was and still it's hard to say I sin good enough
my goose flesh caught his notice.

Kuttawa, Kentucky

A Portion for Foxes

When we was little there was ten of us
fish and loaves the shoes for Sundays
even then the shoes would wear the look
of elder sisters' feet run
down the line so far the cow
ate grass in clear another century.
If there weren't work mama turned
us out to keep the buttermilk from spilling
which was fair as we was like a band of jays
busking gossip for the devil
not the type to turn up drowned
or crushed beneath a barn beam
like some *other* mother's kit.
Wilma was the meanest and the best of us
she told us gullibles of dragonflies thin
and blue they sewed your fingers up together
and she taught us necessary things
like how to borrow dogs' dreams
using Pop's old holed-up hat.
She told us you could catch a thief
by driving nails up in his footprints
waiting good to see a man
who just now caught a limp.
Which we all thought was strange

on account of Wilma taught us no one

here in Dycusburg would lock their doors

besides of course the bootleggers and bank.

When a house was empty

she would take us calling where we knew

there lived the billowingest church hats in their nests.

Which was how we learned the touch

of shoes still had their color

and of rings we didn't tie ourselves

from junegrass and clover.

Wilma hushed up Fay the littlest

with her finest words of murder

and the rest of us she bribed with wisps of

perfume was the only thing

we stole from them the smell of owning

something better than

the hard bones of our feet.

Dycusburg, Kentucky

Garden

To be pretty for you I have dropped
two seeds of turnsole in the dark
of both eyes. I grafted
apple to the quickest
vein in either wrist. I dug a ounce
of poppyseeds where
teeth should be, plugged
my ears with golden balls
of iris. I carved a hole in
either breast to swaddle
dahlias overwinter, like you, so
frightened of the cold.

My mouth grows hot with
purring, with the tunneling of
bees. My tongue, become a catacomb
the wings will fill
with scent.

My skull, for you,
ceramic bowl of flowers you may
hurl against the wall.

I am ready. Lead the way.

The Sawmill

Who joined us to one skin-and-bone
as leaves to a walnut table?

From Grace to Grace, you roll your
seeds into my empty
knothole.

"Our father is the spokeshave,"
you may say. "His shoulders broad, he

skins our days
in long, translucent ribbons.

A child
begins imperfect.

It is his will to scrape us down
to figure."

Grand Rivers, Kentucky

II

Tennessee Valley Authority

The corpse boat split the lilies
in a black and heaving ribbon
in a final day on earth.
This lake ain't lake the way a god
shapes lakes with claws of ice.
A living man remembers when this hole
was not a place of many waters but
a city drowned in just a day.
Underneath the lilies can't you see
the roofs where finches threw a nest
for sowing panic grass and babies.
There was brides made in this place
where herons sweep at corners.
Mudcats breed here now their knowing whiskers
rooted. Home the only thing to root here
in these rooms we cannot save.

Kuttawa, Kentucky

Blue Hole

If I grow my beard long
as this cane
to the fir boards fraying
children's knees—
how will I know myself
from the splinter
in my son's left foot?

How will I know the juice I've spit
from this gum of yellow
skin caught in the rosinweed,
this dead man's fat
flown down the mud cusp?
Where is a man, dead
inside the spaces of himself?
In spring the moss will grow
its hair to brush against
the feet of foxes.

Lyon County, Kentucky

Drunkard's Path

My old mother kneaded bread
newborn gathered at the breast
full as circle skirt
her blue-eyed cotton lap. It was
Wint come drunk he
struck her with the pan as flour
flown to the roof holes and
snowed on me his fists falling like
a basset skull caught the back hoof
of a unbroke horse. Her face so fresh and him so old
he could recall Sherman's burning
trail through Tennessee and when
he left the flour blooming slow as
dust behind a stringer sled.
Last I seen of her was floured
chinbone making
toward me as to point to me. It said
the duty's mine. But yours
it is to carry down
the earth they cleared for you.

Old Nag

Back when she was a living orphan
not the dead one she is now mama called herself
Old Nag she knew it was hers to
heave the weight of all that needed doing like the heft
of telling that old man only
she knew how much man he was inside
his knuckle.

I was newly married in the sight of God a fresh man
on the right side now and money
spent for baby's breath tucked to seem
a new bride not a man's old wife who drags
my children filthy on my train.
Mama there with teeth in and my husband's
father walked me with a veil like it was mine.

Mama came to hate him only after I was wife
his having saved me from such dirt the baby
like a roof hole can't be plugged.

And how to tell her what this man has known
what wickedness he rasps.

The lathe that is his voice.

She died soon after. Froze to death or beat to death still
hoping I would come to something other
than she was.

I was never hers entire.
I will cherish all my freight as gold upon my back.
I will not choose her forty years of wandering
for the nothing I deserve.

Dresden, Tennessee

The Whore of Dycusburg

Rednour girls say I own too many shifts in tints all kinds,
some talk when those girls got two shifts each, one wore down
as cow paths, and the other hid for Sundays, and
what days some Aunt can rustle white cake onto gingham.
    Them girls
only taste liquor for the hot-foot from Lydia's porch to
the church aisle. Now tell me this, what's the good of only seeing
moonshine when it greets you nights taking laundry from the line?
Lydia only got skin for loosing babies in, Fay for running out on,
Wilma for a round of target practice when a man is whiskey drunk.
Now I change shifts by night: halo round the moon, harvest red,
blue for seeing double. With the workmen, I change.
Cotton, silk, skin of a horse, skin of a doe.
Rednour girls feel the wind in one direction, that Easter
blow from the Cumberland side, the one-suit men
who tug their dresses ragged. I make with each
as fields of burley go to clover, cause I love by turns
Andy's good cooking, Gail's burnt temper, Larue's pretty
baby with the sweetwater eyes, and finish off with coffee
to read a bitter truth in. Dregs say one won't live to see his sons
    die young.
One buries a wife in bottle caps. The last goes forgot even by Starla,
our daughter in the white dress. And surely, when I go, they'll find
just a dog's slobber and my upturned palms, but what I got

I didn't string one leaf for, this deep seam of mine, love
rich with color like stones line the walls of heaven,
them tall walls and long roads only Rednour girls pass straight.

Dycusburg, Kentucky

Cast Iron

WOMAN WAS   a turkey beard dazzled on ice-
                   burnt grass

WOMAN WAS   too pretty to break ground

WOMAN WAS   still

WOMAN WAS   like her mother she's a bent nail won't
                   yield to the hammerback

WOMAN WAS   used
to this she saw the sky thin as
                groundwood pages in cheap
                bibles

WOMAN WAS   a snapper knows what the thunder tells her when
                   to loose the hand she loves
                   like food

WOMAN WAS   Leviticus shone in the season
                   of the skillet

WOMAN WAS   a blooded wheel

WOMAN WAS   a saw-whet owl caught between
two screams

WOMAN WAS   who loved the same

WOMAN WAS   burnt
adherent
of the cornbread pan

WOMAN WAS   dissolving slow

Lyon County, Kentucky

Washline

after all the French would invent
a word for drawers to start and finish off an afternoon's
adultery still to know she'll show it and to spot satin
pinned with honest wood pins like she's found
the closest she come to Paris is
flying dirty lace where good boys see it
wives know how to wring
the blood out a sheet if she
could flatten out a man and double him
and beat the footprints off his back still
would she love a shift the way she do
if we could pinch a man by his corner
bleach him every week still
on a cool day running through the halves
of the damp sheets it's so close to cussing each sheet turn
asking for a new world or a better

Dycusburg, Kentucky

Penitent

The prison reaches out
its chimney smoke the dailies
burnt for kindling reach my
mother starching little
collars for days
ain't the Sabbath
the prison seeps.
The children dream of cunning
ladders made of shirts.
The prison soaks the lake
in windows
come unraveled.
Washing taken in by night
she darns the unfamiliar
seams for grandmothers grown
thin-lipped round their missing
teeth.

Eddyville, Kentucky

We Do Not Sing

Don't look like snow. Broomsedge will spill loose the silk. Antlers will
velvet, unvelvet on the branching tree. Seed birds can't know
how many they will be. Each feather springs a new sparrow.
We wait. Cold will soak our feet and watching comes almost
a kind of telling. Wind picks up
the sound of branches cracking way a tall man walks
on land he owns. But no, we're alone here. Each rib
of pignut leaf fights loose. Wind makes the ribs to sing
like smoke through a gray woman's pipe,
so quiet now each blade of
switchgrass underfoot. What's under feet
don't feel. Together we can't tell
what we have given to the listening.

Pin Oak

the mother beat the boy   with dogwood
so to keep him small her   skin
her whole hide tight and yellow
knuckles at the handle of an ax
she slept asleep and standing on the lip
the stairwell high her dress
the color of   a bowstring's
hum

born with switches boy to hide a horse
lame a sheep to stone
a dog to blunt the linnet into   silence
still and light
its bedstraw heart ripped
from the hands
of cedars

bay mare   found him
out her blaze a lonely finger
farmer missing and the boy took up
his house his orchard
bay mare led the sheriff
past coats of bog hemp prairie dock
the farmer   hid inside

a limestone cave his head
dripping splinters

mother chose her seat the day
the pin oak was a scaffold
waiting quiet on his coffin she felt
spite drum in the fibers
in the pine a pedlar's band
of thrum and snap a chant
like burs along her hem a descant
high and thin

                                      the length of rope

III

[the new man bragged]

the new man bragged
said his father owned this land and
knows you by a finger-depth
of oil

his last woman liked talk
if her talk grew he'd take the
screwdriver by its cold end to her
temple

when he dies it won't be
that he dies
the pieces of him split
to chase the groundbirds
out a brushfire

times I wonder if the sound ain't
panthers roaring
underneath
the skim of lakes talk of fish
the crawdad's burrow tells of floods
to come

Kuttawa, Kentucky

The Shrew Ash

Took me time to learn you can't heal in body.
Use the leaves to know a thing
and knowing cuts a pattern
for my skin to meet the junegrass in.
I was told a shrew ash made a cure would seep
down into water feed the ants the flickers eat
and hawks will eat the flickers in the sky a midwife
passing all our faces with her copper feather. I bore us
a hole into a tree
and plugged alive a field mouse
offered it the tree so it would live the way a tree
can pry into the worlds beneath the world.
Can't say it did much reckoning
for what reach I give it.
I cut wands of ash for years for all my scrapes
its twigs not once did stop a hiccup.

Dycusburg, Kentucky

Like as of Fire

Sunday we lay hands
on a girl of ten hand on hand on
cornsilk hair. We sing
the secret language sung
the day the tin roof of the tower beat
on God's floorboard
he got cramp in heaven.
Like our crying and our
fornicating so close to his bed
was so many shrill mice in a pretty
pine floor. To heal
the girl with the crippled up leg
God sends back the song
he took and down it comes
contrary in one mouth as fire
gentle on our bodies as rain.
Soft rain swells the Cumberland
and all her fields in April nuzzles
buttercups the mules won't touch
the crowpoison the wake-robin
the bluets of the field.

Every song got a beat beneath.
Start with the whippoorwill
early meadow colors creep
into the sky. My sons made this
tobacco sled I prime with the jenny
toss the last of the sandlugs for the rest
to thrive. So hot the wasps hang on the honeysuckle
too spent to buzz a sermon.
I know my song remembers
what my fathers told their strings.

Driskill, Kentucky

Odd Fellow's Cross

Old Wayne Peek escaped the penitentiary
had his mother sneak him in a seed
of sunflower hid inside a johnnycake
he watered it beside the lowest prison fence
for sixty days til it was growed so tall
for him to climb it by its leaf
and when he come up to the top
its face spitshined like August
Wayne untucked a sheet he'd stripped from off a cot
and caught himself a breeze his legs full dangling pleased as cuss
and when he got back home his sister give him her old dress
beside a bowl of green persimmons so
our Wayne become a girl an eye as blue as indigo
and one the brown he'd had before
and looking like calamity he wait for all the guards
to come a rattling at the door the meanest one
he asked Wayne for a glass of buttermilk to freshen
up his parch and winked the look of skeletons half-buried so
poor Wayne just smiled his face a blossom of sweet cicely
and spit a quiet hock into his glass
til things got quiet Wayne gone back to Wayne
and no one from the prison found him hid
out deep in Dycusburg among the man-size catfish
in the river and the owls the shape of sowbugs

children keep for toys in matchboxes
on days there's rain and no one free
to tell what's true.

Dycusburg, Kentucky

Fallen Bridge

We knew the land before we knew the land
changed hands cheap.

My great-grandfather digged
up his best wives. The first give him a son
died young and uncomplaining
with room for him
to take another.

Eighty years the bridge grown old.
A ship swum through
and carried it away,
a man's pickup tied to one end
and a redhaired girl to the other, bit
like a weak bone in cold.

Before it was
the land would pace
back to back, way two men
like to shoot
but for a word hung in the air.

Echo

I lost

them farmers and their barren
mules they barely kept a Tail Holt
here on living and *the second*
there was corn there was a *child*
to come devouring *This*
is blood-deep ground My wife's old *country*
become my own but I was
made in dry dust come to know
my father by the files my mother
sewed up in my britches
as I passed into San Quentin
with my lily freckles
each my ears the size of cock's *plumes*

Yes I hear you Wife

like

I said I reel the whiskey stories that *a man*
should never own God bless the
dancing girl gone green here *on my*
arm could tell you of the inside
of boxcars I prefer the *back*

side of regret When my mother
lost me I rode rails
so young a nip of rye will *best*
the best of fires
But the navy brung me salt
prairies and a loan to *make*
a wife with drape
my gold about her neck
the halfmoons in her nails was
blue as chicory *the knot*
we tied so *tight*
come night
no rifle could untie it

Kuttawa, Kentucky

Father

it's god's grace he's alive but
the life he made tells you he
won't stick around to wonder
what a man does with a face
lost a cockfight to himself
each night his legs less limb more
memory and fewer in a day
each fish he scales
become the same fish
every vein become one gully
what's left to touch the light
behind the cataract
carrot flower aflame
pond traps the last light
the bass skims its fire
for supper

Kuttawa, Kentucky

Topping the Flower

Paul said evermore, rejoice
not just with my nut-hard finger
to the frets, but with my jenny at my side,
yoked and suckering in August.
Rejoice with toothache, and the pick
I culled to cure it from the poplar lightning
struck. Pray without ceasing, means
my cheek to the cow's dusk flank,
good barn one season, bad house,
and rags enough to hide from wind.
The youngest gives thanks
for a dress full sewed, color of meadowsweet.
There are days my hat brim's hole
catches sun inside its little round,
a clean snare for God's hind leg,
I study things a minute.
The writing on a worm-chewed leaf,
what colors light can throw on sand,
poison sumac curling round the oak
like three-tooth serpents.
Rejoice to harrow, rejoice to string,

the pastor and the auctioneer sing, but sing

like men who wait for rain.

Driskill, Kentucky

Hillis Rednour Meets a Leviathan

We love our neighbors til the neighbors
spit tobacco juice down Hoptown
way a locust would that's
cupped inside a hand.

The hand that cut our leaf
killed a boy for spitting
in the wrong man's bucket
dragged him half his head shot off
through Greenbriar Swamp.
Down Lamasco man who done
the killing lay a week
beneath a woman's bonnet low from
laws no one
thought much of.

Some black masks come
for Hillis. Hillis better loved a
jug to splitting wood with children
knee-high looking
lean his Ruth six months round her
ankles each hedge-apple thick.

Yoked his ankles to a horse and tore
him through the bramble
made the stones to hurl
their weight and sassafras to
switch. Honeysuckles throwed mouthfuls
of sleeping bees and grace alone no
cottonmouth come out the kerf of rivers.

At light they give him to his door and
promises to kill him if his children didn't
fatten. Could be that his Ruth has loved
him for the harrowing. Still
I do not know
what beast drug him,
what man held the reins.

IV

Eclogue

couldn't say who it was shouldered her
the spent side of January
not a nightbird squalling
shook apart the ice
it drew so near her
she mistook it
for a tender thing

Dresden, Tennessee

His Left Foot

boy learnt   what he'd learn when
he wanted   he was taught still
to forgive   before he grew tall
enough   to know a man
would take   a part of him for
nothing   keeps nothing but
still be   his father

Murray, Kentucky

Solomon's Seal

Can't leave marks upon him can't run
books beneath the horse's
foot rub the spine with
corpse hands. Might hide the words
in blackgum trees to give my feel of him
a life. Ring to ring, the hate should hold him
longer than a man can live. The finger
of the law don't care
what it is he done, no man hurts
for all the names he
corked up in his bottle.
We will die this way.
But I got scratches buried in the ground
to claw their way to them
skins that draw what's hidden
from what's seen. Burn the
white and lean, as flowers
know the time to ruin
the day their good's
been done.

Murray, Kentucky

Third Story Fall

we	killed	him	when	
we	loved	him	when	he lied to us the women he could have
we	loved	him	when	he told us what there was of little
			when	he died he still was pretty teeth so tall
			when	he died he was little more than railing
he	loved	us	when	he died
he	killed	us	when	the ants gathered what pollen he had
he	killed	us		in so many patterns

Paducah, Kentucky

[Back when people died it was clean]

Back when people died it was clean
beneath a wheel a hoof
the loose bone
of a raised barn or slow
so slow you'd barely spot the difference
as a woman spent her last
words into her saucer of beef tea.

Who blows a hole clear through his own heart?
No one there but bullbats and the frogs.
Them singing like the boy's too good
to hold in hand singing like
you can't suck spun sugar as
what's on the tongue is real but only
just. You find it hard to recollect the taste.

Boy never had sense to pound sand into a rat hole so
they loved him for the nothing
where the sense should be.
His daddy joined him on
the highway before he'd woke to
the dark of morning. It took ten years
to strip the sheets from the bed was his.
To dump the ashes out. Our plates

was next to empty then and none of us could
sing a note that deaf cat
at the organ tinkering an extra verse alone.
Sung like branchwater dripping and
no hands to meet the drops.

Grand Rivers, Kentucky

Lot's Wife

My son has holed himself upstairs,
locked door, the glass bowl
overflows with
brightleaf ash.

He won't be hungry yet, I fixed
a plate in early March
cured in smoke we pass from lung to lung
through the walls of this house.

He writes me notes at night
in backs of broken ornaments,
in redbud limbs I read
with the grit of my teeth.

His daddy can't love right.
That love tuned to notes
the cats and I hear trilling in the wall,
love I pack like salt to ice.

What he knows are hollow sounds.
When vacancy lit our son's ribs
the length of his life.
The consolations we tucked in

the sheets of his pine bed.
What that bullet took
when it came
to collect.

Grand Rivers, Kentucky

Riddle

I was born
I died in
one breath
one sound

what I am
born cold
came hot then the
hot came cold

I had one
tooth I was the
tooth he pulled

I am what
I left behind
I left behind a
nothing

but the salt
they threw
to hide
what they
forgot

what I am
the vermin
burrowed through
when the bucket
came too hot

what am I
what came before
the pinpoint
before what's after

Grand Rivers, Kentucky

V

Hognose Snake

The hognose snake has two lines
of defense to cast her backbone tall
like there's fight left in her
or to feign abjection
bare the mildew of her belly
furl her tongue into a beggar's
cup. The hognose thrills her
nose to rotting
sycamore leaf. The hawk will finger
frets upon the limb. To be contemptible
is hers. The final pleasure of the cornered thing.
To face together mirrors
make a life in what they see
as Mother touches flame to the living
room carpet. To know its brightest possibility.
Its godlike shimmer.

Dresden, Tennessee

The Shrike Took His Name for Crying

a fork stood in her breastbone
marked the spot he meant to carve
his wife to something useful

he walled the house in brambles white
sawtooth come to berries come to
wingbeats in the summer
like gates could fly

he hung a sparrow
on the honey locust thorn
it was a portion for another day
for autumn feathered red
and lined in golden ribs

Kuttawa, Kentucky

Familiars

One cat became five,
five became nine.
Then a flood and ebb
as each moon brought its tide
below the trailer floor,
the cedar ledge,
or looped inside the pumpkin vine.
A litter died
beneath the sumac trees
where mists and nettles brimmed.
Still more hid in sedge,
to pick off sunning skinks
and redpolls sowing seeds.
Come summer, cats followed
premonitions, skimmed
the runoff creeks, the hollow
down the railroad track
where we palmed pocketfuls
of anthracite: Pearl, Abel,
Willow, Changeling,
Spitfire the stray.
As Mother told me time
to go, the baby's coming soon

and no man here to claim him,
all the beasts fled overnight.

Kuttawa, Kentucky

To Field Dress a Doe

Step 1. Begin with the feel of a desecration. Cut below her udder, around the anus and remove, wary not to pierce the bladder. This will feel you've killed her twice.

Step 2. Split the muscle of the pelvis. Open her to the rasp of broom sedge.

Step 3. Ease your knife through the muscle wall. Draw her skin like a warm, blood curtain to shield her guts from rupture. Draw until you find the breastbone.

Step 4. By now, the birds are calling to the likelihood of morning.

Step 5. Do not spare her cape for beauty. Slice to the chin and loose what you find.

Step 6. With a toothed blade, split her pelvic bone, sapling-like and supple.

Step 7. Drag from the windpipe down, removing all that was inside her in as few strokes as you can.

Step 8. If there is a child, place the heart into her hands. Tell her this is necessary.

Step 9. Turn her over. Across a log, if you find one. Across an oak, if you find one.

Step 10. The oakmoss holds her blood. It scents the wood with the stone weight of your hunger.

[his name]

his name   drapes on my head

                  weaves me bright

his name   what moths see

                  in the windowglass

his name   he carries loose to roll

                  into earth

his name   everything he gave this

                  water splits the hill

his name   tapers til it finds

his name

Black Swallowtail

little sister

to be swallowed is to be   SEEN   to be beautiful on bishop weed

   your slip   SEEN   to a sharp point the fire reaches bluest

   in heat   DRAWN   you forget

yourself in air   DRAWN   away away you've hardly

aloft your one lash   BEATEN   one wing still exquisite

nickers after sugar   BEATEN   soft as a horse

   already   today what saps

   tomorrow   EATEN   stonecrop and the quartervine

   SWEETEN   every flower

is a cup you will not   DRAIN   again each redbud

just a town you won't   revisit

For M. W.
Murray, Kentucky

Great Blue Heron

filly-tall cow-slow don't
say how many days
he'll gullet still he
throws a shadow on the lake
catch what he catch til
no one finds him warshed
up grinning as death comes funny
to the flat possum
like he guards the hole to hell
a crawdad digged him up
looking for the coldest mud
but blue a color won't sink
into god's flesh why
it's gone the color of a cruel eye
why I never found one feather
heard the cry he make
still holding none but the spindle
was his leg when sun caught
my eye too sharp to see

Murray, Kentucky

Chicken Hawk

put strychnine on
the heads of
new chicks won't
know no different after while
no chicken hawk
will touch you no
more—less one or two
the smallest

it's good to be
the chicken hawk
spreads his feathers til
they barely touch the bird
like stars that chain
the bear together

his feet scaled in
every ornery snake he eat
six days out of seven
he knows what to grasp

some days better

be a man

but a man

his corked bottle loosed

where mercy don't grow

Driskill, Kentucky

Box Turtle

we hid my brother in the box turtle

           to watch minnows

           swill the water

           for futures

we stowed my brother

           to hear water striders

           skim yellow

           from the pond's edge

we made his bed

           where swallows could not steal

           one straw

           to make their purples

           on the slopes of night

such a night he may

           carve a door

                Murray, Kentucky

NOTES

"Chamber": My grandmother once witnessed my grandfather playing drunk, solitary Russian roulette after returning from a shift at the candy store.

"Even Shorn": Song of Solomon 4:2: "Thy teeth are like a flock of sheep that are even shorn, which came up from the washing; whereof every one bear twins, and none is barren among them."

"Blue Hole": This is a Night Rider term for a body of water in which the body of a man is concealed forever. This often referred to racial terror, but also to the disposal of those who opposed organized anti-monopolist efforts in the tobacco industry.

"Drunkard's Path": Quilt patterns frequently assume sinister titles, perhaps because they allow women to see the patterns of their lives sub specie aeternitatis.

"The Whore of Dycusburg": The speaker of this poem, whom my mother still calls "the whore of Dycusburg," was not a sex worker, but was so maligned for the duration of her life. She supposedly enjoyed relations with several of my great-uncles in a town so small it has no local law enforcement. Once, my grandmother retrieved my grandfather from one of his benders to find him crawling on all fours in this woman's front yard, wearing nothing but one of her many shifts.

"Like as of Fire": The speaker of this poem, my great-grandfather, was an illiterate tobacco tenant farmer; "his mark" listed on his draft papers does not improve between WWI and WWII. Between those wars, he joined the Pentecostal church and learned to speak God's language.

"Echo": Tail Holt was once a town in Western Kentucky, so named because its citizens barely kept a "tail holt," or tail-hold, on survival. This is also true of the second speaker in this poem, who pieces the scraps of her husband's words like feed sack.

"His Left Foot": My brother's brother lost half his foot at the age of two, when their alcoholic father ran him over with a riding mower. He is now, I believe, a martial arts instructor.

"Solomon's Seal": The rhizome of the Solomon's seal flower, which I used to pick as a child, supposedly resembles the Hebrew lettering on King Solomon's seal. This lettering is actually scarring from the broken end of the leaf stalk.

"Third Story Fall": My cousin, who lived simultaneously inside and outside his Paducah closet, died in his midthirties. He fell directly onto his skull from a third-story balcony.

"[Back when people died it was clean]": My cousin shot himself in the heart at the age of twenty-two.

"Riddle": The "solution," for those who need it, is the bullet with which my cousin shot himself.

ACKNOWLEDGMENTS

My grateful acknowledgment to the editors of publications where poems previously appeared.

Colorado Review: "Garden," and "Great Blue Heron"

december: "Odd Fellow's Cross"

Peripheries: "Father" and "To Field Dress a Doe"

South Carolina Review: "A Portion for Foxes"

Split Rock Review: "Tennessee Valley Authority" and "The Shrew Ash"

Tupelo Quarterly: "The Sawmill"

To my husband, thank you for support and infinite patience.

To my mother, who wrote this book with me.

To Jorie Graham, whom I cannot possibly thank enough.

To Juan Felipe Herrera, who cannot write a bad sentence.

To Michelle Taylor, my secret agent.

To Sarah Gorham, whose ear for music is incomparable.

To Josh Bell, whose workshop woke me up.

Isabel Duarte-Gray was born in Oakland, California, and raised in a trailer in Kuttawa, Kentucky. She is currently a PhD candidate at Harvard University, where she studies Latinx literature, poetry, and ecocriticism. She received her BA in English and Russian from Amherst College. Her poems have appeared or are forthcoming in *Colorado Review*, *Bat City Review*, *South Carolina Review*, and *december*, among others.

SARABANDE BOOKS is a nonprofit literary press located in Louisville, KY. Founded in 1994 to champion poetry, short fiction, and essay, we are committed to creating lasting editions that honor exceptional writing. For more information, please visit sarabandebooks.org.